Live Better Yoga

Live Better Yoga

exercises and inspirations for well-being

Tara Fraser

BARNES
&NOBLE
B O O K S
NEW YORK

Live Better: Yoga
Tara Fraser

For David, Marion, Nina and Guy, with love.

This edition published by Barnes & Noble, Inc.
by arrangement with Duncan Baird Publishers

2003 Barnes & Noble

M 10 9 8 7 6 5 4 3 2 1

ISBN: 0-7607-4921-3

Conceived, created and designed by
Duncan Baird Publishers Ltd
Sixth Floor, Castle House
75–76 Wells Street
London W1T 3QH

Managing Editor: Judy Barratt
Editor: Louise Nixon
Managing Designer: Manisha Patel
Designer: Clare Thorpe
Picture Research: Cee Weston-Baker
Commissioned Photography: Matthew Ward

Library of Congress Cataloging-in-Publication
Data is available.

Typeset in Filosofia and Son Kern
Colour reproduction by Scanhouse, Malaysia
Printed and bound in Thailand by Sirivatana
Interprint (SI)

Publisher's notes
Before following any advice or practice suggested
in this book, it is recommended that you consult
your doctor as to its suitability, especially if
you suffer from any health problems or special
conditions. The publishers, the author and the
photographers cannot accept any responsibility
for any injuries or damage incurred as a result of
following the exercises in this book, or of using
any of the therapeutic methods described or
mentioned here.

The abbreviations BCE and CE are used throughout
this book. BCE means Before the Common Era
(equivalent to BC); CE means of the Common Era
(equivalent to AD).

contents

INTRODUCTION

As a yoga teacher I see many people in their weekly classes gaining great benefits from yoga – their posture improves, their breathing deepens and slows and they become more at ease in their bodies. However, I also know that when life is at its most demanding and all your resources are channelled into coping with stress, yoga may well be last thing you think about doing. Yet this is exactly when yoga can help you the most. If you think that you are too busy or too stressed to do yoga, this little book is for you!

This book gives you all you need to begin to make yoga part of your everyday life: a little background information; some simple postures, breathing and meditation exercises to try; and a selection of quotations to inspire you. Practising a few postures each day can release neck and shoulder tension, reduce back pain and make you feel comfortable in your body again. Doing a simple relaxation exercise when you get home from work can stop you taking your work worries into your home life. Spending a few minutes in quiet meditation before bedtime can improve the quality of your sleep. These practices are not difficult to learn by yourself. Once you have tried them and have experienced their benefits, you will wonder how you coped without them!

Most importantly, yoga is not just about practising postures: it is a practical method for making life better all round. If you are too stiff or too unwell to do the postures in this book, try the breathing and meditation exercises in Chapter Three, or perhaps make some changes to your diet as recommended in Chapter Four. All of these suggestions are part of yoga, and they can help you to develop a more positive attitude to life and to bring balance and harmony to your mind and body.

The exercises you see in this book are developed from my own daily practice. They are not particularly tough, demanding or athletic. They are simply what I have found I need to live better through yoga. I offer them to you here, with thanks to the people who have taught me and with the hope that you may find something to help you live better through yoga, too.

Chapter One

yoga Know-how

Yoga is an ancient tradition that originated more than 2,000 years ago as a means by which humankind could attain self-realization, or enlightenment. Yoga has a mixed image in the West: on the one hand it is seen as mystical and esoteric; on the other, as simply an exercise system. In practice, yoga techniques begin with the health of the physical body as a route to improving the state of mental, emotional and ultimately spiritual well-being. Yoga includes the practice of postures and breathing exercises that, despite their antiquity, are of special relevance to modern people for they form a balanced and holistic approach to countering the stresses and strains of our lives.

You may begin to do yoga because you want to develop greater flexibility in your limbs, or because you want to achieve a greater sense of tranquillity, or because you are seeking some kind of spiritual understanding. Whatever your reason for starting your yoga practice, you will soon find that yoga becomes an important and enjoyable part of your everyday life.

In this chapter we look at the origins and aims of yoga. There is practical advice on how to approach the postures, breathing and meditations. Read this chapter before you attempt any of the exercises in the book – it will help you understand how to do the postures safely and how to get the most out of your practice.

WHAT IS YOGA?

Yoga dates back thousands of years, to the time of the Vedic culture – around 2800BCE. Having developed as one of India's philosophical traditions, yoga has continued to evolve through generations of teachers and practitioners. As a result, many variations of yoga have developed over the centuries. One particular variation, Hatha yoga, has gained huge popularity in the West as a means to relax and improve health. Hatha yoga uses a combination of physical postures, cleansing methods and breathing exercises to focus the mind in preparation for meditation and the path of yoga called Raja (royal) yoga.

For most people the word yoga conjures up the image of someone sitting in the lotus position looking peaceful. However, *yoga* can be translated as "union" or, more elaborately, as "tying the strands of the mind together". In fact, Patanjali, author of the *Yoga Sutras* (c.200BCE–c.200CE) gives the definition of yoga as *yogasgcittavrttinirodhah*, which roughly translates as "yoga is the ability to focus the mind on a single point without distraction". No mention of the lotus position! While yoga is a physical discipline, it uses the body and breathing to develop self-awareness and mental clarity.

In the modern West many people are obsessed with the body. It is hardly surprising then that we have seized upon the practice with such enthusiasm – it does undoubtedly promote a better-looking, healthier body. However, the wonderful – and most important – thing about yoga is that its benefits include a calmer, more focused mind. When you begin to practise yoga, you may be interested only in the physical benefits – they provide good motivation! However, before long, you may find that yoga postures lift your mood and improve your state of mind. After several months of regular practice, you may even feel that you gain a clearer perspective on life. If this happens you have entered a different phase of your yoga practice and it is now time for you to release any preoccupation with the body and begin your journey of inward reflection. Read the following two pages for the ten best reasons for bringing yoga into your life.

TEN GOOD REASONS TO PRACTISE YOGA

1 Yoga is not just for athletes, popstars and supermodels! Yoga is for everyone: young or old, male or female, healthy or sick. Yoga can always be adapted to your individual needs, whatever your circumstances.

2 Even if you are facing many challenges in life, it is easy to start doing yoga and you will experience instant benefits, such as stress-relief. Furthermore, once you begin to practise regularly, yoga will help you to live your life with renewed positivity and enthusiasm.

3 Yoga is safe. Where other forms of exercise might put a strain on your heart, muscles and joints, yoga, practised properly (with an awareness of your physical limitations), is a completely harmless form of exercise.

4 Yoga needs no special equipment. While there are a few props that might make your practice more comfortable, the only thing you really need in order to do yoga is you.

5 Yoga both tones the respiratory system and helps you to breathe more fully, deeply and easily (thus increasing your oxygen intake), which, in turn, will improve your physical and mental well-being.

6 Yoga improves the efficiency of your body systems, aiding digestion, the assimilation of nutrients and the elimination of toxins.

7 Yoga improves the quality of your sleep so that, when you wake up, you feel refreshed and full of vitality.

8 Yoga gives you energy and helps you to channel your energy effectively so that you don't waste it on tension, stress and negativity.

9 Through practising yoga techniques, you experience a genuine sense of outward tranquillity, which eventually helps you achieve a deep state of inner peace, too.

10 Yoga is FUN!

Pranayama [breath control] is
the regulation of the inhalation, exhalation
and suspension of the breath. By observing
the length and duration of these phases,
you can make the breath long and subtle.

PATANJALI

YOGA SUTRAS (*C.*200BCE–*C.*200CE)

The posture should be both steady and soft.

PATANJALI

YOGA SUTRAS (*C.*200BCE–*C.*200CE)

WHAT STYLE OF YOGA IS BEST FOR ME?

Hatha yoga, the variation of yoga most widely known in the West, has many different "branches". Each of these branches has a distinct style with a different emphasis and specific characteristics. However, all styles of yoga are practised with the same ultimate aim – that of self-realization through both the body and the mind.

In practical terms, you may find that one particular style of yoga suits you better than another, depending on the type of person you are and the kind of lifestyle you lead. When choosing a style to practise, follow your instinct and the advice of a yoga teacher whom you trust and respect. Below is a simple description of just a few of the most commonly offered styles of Hatha yoga.

Iyengar yoga A physically demanding and anatomically exact method of yoga developed by one of the twentieth century's foremost teachers, B.K.S. Iyengar. Posture is taught to a high level before other techniques (such as breathing) are introduced. Props, such as blankets, blocks and belts, can be used to adapt the postures to individual needs. Iyengar yoga can make an excellent therapeutic practice for the injured or sick.

Astanga vinyasa yoga A method of yoga consisting of several series of set posture sequences. Each posture is linked to the next by a *vinyasa* (a linking movement) creating a continuous flow. The "primary series" (the first series) is physically demanding, and continuous use of *ujjayi* breathing heats the body, making this a deeply purifying practice.

Sivananda Yoga Swami Sivananda developed this technique and it was introduced to thousands in the West in the 1950s. Spiritual teaching, chanting, meditation, breathing techniques, and dietary and other advice supplement posture practice. Classes can vary but a resting position is often suggested after each posture.

Viniyoga This method was developed by T.K.V. Desikachar in the 1960s. Taught principally either one-on-one or in small groups, Viniyoga is ideal for those seeking therapeutic benefits from yoga. Teachers offer postures, breathing techniques, philosophy and chanting based on the individual constitution of the student.

FIVE BODIES – LINKING THE MIND, BODY AND SPIRIT

According to yogic theory, the body is just the outside "sheath" of the self. This external, physical body has four other interconnecting layers that constitute the "subtle" body. The physical and the subtle bodies are collectively known as the *panca-kosha*, or "five sheaths":

1 *Annamaya kosha* – the food sheath, the physical body;
2 *Pranamaya kosha* – the energetic system;
3 *Manomaya kosha* – the mind sheath, the part of the mind that processes information and helps us function on a basic level;
4 *Vijnanamaya kosha* – the intellectual sheath, the aspect of the mind that allows higher levels of understanding;
5 *Anandamaya kosha* – the bliss sheath, the part of us that connects us with the universal consciousness.

Although many of us are willing to accept the idea that the mind, body and spirit do not operate in isolation from one another, we often lack any practical means by which to encourage them to work together to enhance our well-being. The practice of Hatha yoga offers a way to link these multiple aspects of the whole person — through posture and breathing. *Asanas* (postures) cleanse, strengthen and purify the physical body; improve the flow of energy to the limbs and vital organs in the energetic body; and can lead to improved focus, concentration and analytical powers in the mind.

In yoga *prana* is the name given to the vital force that exists both within us and in the world around us. Breath is said to be the interface between the physical body and the mind. *Pranayama* (breath control) influences the flow of *prana* in our body. Dedicated *asana* practice brings about changes in our breathing, making it possible to manipulate the breathing in *pranayama* practice to a subtle level. Deliberately changing the speed, depth and duration of your breath can have a profound effect on your mind at a simple level (*manomaya kosha*) and at a higher level (*vijnanamaya kosha*). Together *asana* and *pranayama* help us to sense the bliss sheath (*anandamaya kosha*) and so connect with the universal consciousness throughout our daily lives.

THE PRACTICALITIES OF YOGA

All you need to practise yoga is a small space and a little time. Ideally you would have enough space to roll out a yoga mat and about forty minutes to an hour to practise. But it is possible to do some yoga practice in other circumstances: for example, a gentle twist to relieve backache at the office or a standing pose, such as mountain pose, while waiting for a train. Initially you should just adapt yoga to fit into your life. Once you begin to feel the benefits from your practice, you will be able to decide if you would like to commit more time to yoga. Below are some general guidelines for your yoga practice:

- Wear loose, comfortable clothes that enable you to move easily. Remove your watch and any jewelry.
- Go barefoot – this gives you a sense of close contact with the ground and allows the muscles in your feet to operate freely.
- Leave at least two to three hours after a heavy meal before beginning your practice. The best time to practise is in the morning before breakfast.

- A yoga mat is helpful but not essential. You may want a blanket to cushion you from a hard floor. Attending a class is certainly the easiest way to learn yoga; however, practising at home by yourself will help to develop anything that you have learned in class.

- If you do have access to classes, try to select one with a teacher whom you like. It is far better to go infrequently to a class taught by someone whom you find inspiring, than go regularly to a class taught by someone whom you find unsympathetic or demotivating.

- If you are pregnant, unwell or have disabilities, find a teacher who can adapt the practice for your needs.

- Finally, and most importantly, yoga is not supposed to hurt! If you feel unwell, exhausted or unsettled as a result of any of your practice, you are either doing something wrong or the practice is inappropriate for you at that time. You must be constantly observant and mindful of how you feel during your practice, both at home and in a class. Notice the "detail" of your yoga practice and be aware of any subtle changes in how you feel. Be fully "present" in your yoga.

HOW TO PRACTISE POSTURES

Yoga postures are designed to cleanse, tone and purify the body, which in turn affects the mind and your ability to practise *pranayama* and meditation without distraction. There are also many health benefits from practising postures: improved flexibility, stamina, strength and balance; better functioning of your nervous and endocrine systems and internal organs; and enhanced quality of your breathing. In addition, you will have greater focus, concentration and clarity of mind.

In order to gain these benefits, postures should be practised mindfully and sensibly. The postures in chapters Two and Three of this book form two complete practices lasting approximately thirty minutes each. Chapter Two contains mostly expanding, opening or uplifting postures, which can help you feel more energetic. The poses in Chapter Three are mostly closing, folding or bowing-down poses, which encourage introspection and relaxation – they are ideal if you are suffering from stress and tension (however, avoid them if you are depressed). Try to keep the following tips in mind when practising these or any other yoga postures:

- Choose poses that seem appropriate to your mood and energy level. Each time you practise, begin with gentler poses and work up to stronger ones.
- Breathe evenly and slowly through your nose throughout the postures. Generally try to lift, lengthen and extend the body as you inhale; use each exhalation to find stability, balance and ease.
- Never rush into or out of a posture – try to be mindful of every phase of the posture, and take your time to move softly but purposefully to the next stage.
- Never strain in a pose – if it hurts, stop.
- As you practise, check for unnecessary tension in your body – especially in your face, hands, feet and buttocks.
- Don't habitually practise in front of a mirror. Focus on how the posture feels, not what it looks like. Try to release from your mind's eye any image of "perfection".
- Patanjali, author of the *Yoga Sutras* (*c.*200BCE–*c.*200CE), taught that the postures should be both *sthira* (steady or firm) and *sukha* (soft). Try to make them so!

HOW TO PRACTISE BREATHING

In yoga the breath is said to connect the mind and the body (see page 19). The power of breathing practice (*pranayama*) to change your state of mind is extremely strong. For this reason you must progress slowly and carefully – never strain your breathing in *pranayama*. If you feel dizzy or light-headed, return to your normal breathing immediately. If you suffer from any respiratory problems, such as asthma, you should practise under a teacher who can guide you.

A breathing practice can last anything from two minutes to half an hour or more. However, if you are new to yoga begin with a three-minute practice once or twice a day – you will be surprised by what a challenge it is to concentrate on the breath for even a short while.

At first you could practise *pranayama* lying down – especially if you are unwell or fatigued. In time aim to sit upright with your spine straight. You might try sitting toward the edge of a firm chair with your feet flat on the floor, or cross-legged on the floor.

HOW TO PRACTISE MUDRAS

*Mudra*s are positions (mostly of the hands) that affect the body's energetic system and the flow of *prana* (life energy) within it. You will find that *mudra*s are safe and easy to learn and use and they can enhance your mood quite quickly once you become sensitive to them.

There are four different kinds of *mudra* explained in this book, all of which have different effects, such as improved stability or increased energy. You can either use the same *mudra* for several minutes at a time, two or three times a day, or you can simply practise a *mudra* as you feel you need it – for example, to calm yourself while you are commuting on crowded public transport, or to help you to gather your thoughts before a job interview.

The best time to practise *mudra*s, however, is during the sitting phase after a posture and breathing session. Close your eyes as you practise a *mudra* and allow your attention to turn inward. Don't try hard – simply allow your fingers to touch lightly, and allow your mind and body to be still and quiet.

25

HOW TO PRACTISE MEDITATION

For meditation to be effective, you ought to practise regularly, but don't practise at all without the guidance of a teacher if you are depressed. Set aside a special time and place for your meditation practice – your mind focuses more easily when you establish a routine.

You should sit in an upright position for meditation unless you are too ill or weak to do so – most of us will drift into sleep if we attempt to meditate lying down! Choose a position in which you can sit comfortably without fidgeting – this will probably mean sitting on a hard, straight-backed chair or a low stool, at least to begin with. If you can sit comfortably in a traditional meditation pose, such as a basic cross-legged position or half-lotus posture, you should do so. (For half-lotus posture, sit on the floor and bend your left knee so that the heel of your left foot comes to rest near your groin and your outer thigh and calf rest on the floor. Place your right foot on your left thigh, as close as possible to your hip-socket. Prop your right knee up with a block if you wish.)

Take steps to minimize the number of distractions that might occur during your meditation practice. For example, turn off your mobile telephone, unplug your landline and close the doors of your meditation room to make it as quiet as possible. If you like, make a simple altar by placing some flowers or some uplifting pictures on a low table – doing so will help to draw your attention in toward a single focus.

You will find two step-by-step meditation exercises later in this book (see pages 65 and 101), which focus on energy centres, or *chakra*s, in your body. When you first start to practise meditation, you will find it difficult to stop the stream of thoughts that endlessly pass through your head – you might start thinking about the day ahead or last night's television show. However, after a period of regular practice you should find you are able to focus more easily, let go of the clutter in your mind and eventually create the still, single focus of the mind characteristic of deep meditation. Reaching this goal may take years of practice but the process of getting there is beneficial and rewarding in itself.

Crown chakra – sahasrara

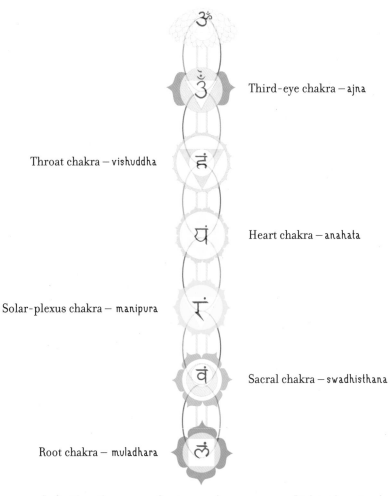

Third-eye chakra – ajna

Throat chakra – vishuddha

Heart chakra – anahata

Solar-plexus chakra – manipura

Sacral chakra – swadhisthana

Root chakra – muladhara

Left side – ida   Centre – sushumna   Right side – pingala

YOUR BODY'S ENERGY CENTRES
Chakras

Prana passes through a system of energy channels (*nadis*) which intersect at various places to form "wheels" of spinning energy, known as *chakras*. There are seven *chakras* along the vertical axis of the body. Each *chakra* is represented by a particular colour and sound; various qualities and attributes are associated with each one. The diagram opposite shows the *chakras* and connections between the three principal *nadis*: *ida*, *pingala* and *sushumna*. The condition of your *chakra* system can be known only through careful observation and consistent yoga practice.

Yoga postures and breathing exercises help to clear the *nadis* for *prana* to move through them freely. Meditation on a particular *chakra* can bring about better flow of energy through it, balancing the areas associated with it. The two meditations in this book are based around the root *chakra*, or *muladhara* (page 65), and the heart *chakra*, or *anahata* (page 101).

Like two golden birds perched on a tree,
United companions are the ego and the Self.
One eats the sweet and sour fruits of the tree
While the other looks on without eating.

Thinking we are the ego,
We feel attached and fall into sorrow.
But realize that you are the Self,
and you will be freed from sorrow.
When you realize that you are the Self,
Supreme source of light and love,
You transcend good and evil
And move into a state of union.

BHAGAVAD GITA (6TH CENTURY BCE)

Chapter Two

yoga energy

Aspects of modern life can make us feel drained and exhausted: many people routinely juggle pressurized working conditions, long commuting distances and family commitments. Mobile telephones and e-mail further consume our time and energy. It is little wonder that we often come home from work worn out.

But help is at hand: yoga is a brilliant energizer! The postures and other techniques stimulate your body's energetic system to make you feel more alive.

This chapter includes postures, breathing practices and meditations that help to pep up a lethargic system, as well as ones that channel energy to specific parts of your body. Some of the postures require a little energy to execute; others are gentle. Simple breathing techniques take only a few minutes. Energy generated through meditation can support you through difficult periods in your life, such as changing job, moving home or becoming a parent.

You can use the techniques in this chapter in two ways. Try them in sequence, in the order given, to create an energizing yoga practice lasting about thirty minutes (take a few breaths in each posture). Or select a few postures that suit your mood and spend a little time in each one, keeping your breathing steady and smooth; meditate and practise *mudra* for as long as you feel comfortable.

YOGA BRINGS YOU ENERGY

Before you begin your yoga practice, it is important to understand how the postures, breathing and meditations of yoga can bring you energy.

In many Western exercise systems, energy is thought of as something to be used up – we talk of expending energy to burn calories. However, the yogic understanding of energy is not related to burning calories at all – in yoga, energy is related to a subtle force called *prana*. This subtle energy is said to flow through all living things. *Prana* flows through a network of channels in our body called *nadi*s. Special centres of energy known as *chakra*s (see pages 28–9) are formed where the *nadi*s intersect (at certain points along the body).

Meditation on the *chakra*s – and the practice of postures – can assist the flow of *prana*, which is a positive result of yoga practice. When we are well, *prana* circulates freely throughout our energetic system. When we are sick, *prana* is being lost from the body and, consequently, we feel depleted of energy.

Try this simple exercise to feel the flow of *prana* in your body: bring your hands together as if in prayer. Keeping the tips of your fingers and thumbs together, move the heels of your hands away from one another, so that your palms part and just the tips of your fingers and thumbs are touching. This is a *mudra* (see page 25). This gesture allows a flow of *prana* through your fingertips, which in turn creates a circuit of energy through your body. You might be surprised by how clear-headed the *mudra* can make you feel. Hold this position for as long as you feel comfortable.

According to yoga there are three qualities that pervade everything: *rajas* (energy), *tamas* (inertia) and *satwa* (clarity). Often our lives are out of balance and we swing between highs of energy and lows of exhaustion. Through yoga we aim to try to bring our lives into a state of harmony and clarity (*satwa*). In this chapter the practices are intended to free the flow of *prana* through your system to help you to feel more constant, more in balance. (If you feel you always lack energy, the suggestions in Chapter Three will help you to conserve *prana*.)

MOUNTAIN POSE VARIATIONS
Tadasana

Variation 1

1   Stand feet hip-width apart and parallel. Lengthen your torso, relax your shoulders and draw your chin slightly toward your throat to lengthen your neck.

2   Breathing in, move your arms out in front of you and lift them over your head, simultaneously raising your heels as far as you comfortably can. Find your balance. Exhale and return to position 1. Repeat six times.

Variation 2

1   Stand with the inner edges of your feet touching. Bring the palms of your hands together in front of your chest.

2   Inhale, lift your arms out to the sides and bring your palms together over your head. Exhale and draw your arms down to return to position 1. Repeat six times.

Try these variations of mountain pose (either in sequence or individually) to improve your balance and stability.

Variation 1

Variation 2

1   2   1   2

MINI SUN SALUTATION

1 Stand with your feet hip-width apart and parallel.

2 Breathing in, lift your arms out to the sides and up until your palms face each other directly over your shoulders.

3 Breathing out, bend forward and bring your arms out to the sides and down to touch either your shins or the floor. Bend your knees as much as you need to.

4 Inhale, broaden your chest and lengthen your spine as much as you can. Keep your neck in line with your spine but look upward. Then exhale, relax your torso, head and neck and return to position 3. Inhale, then move your arms out to the sides and over your shoulders and lift your body back to position 2. Exhale, relax your arms to your sides and return to position 1. Repeat the whole sequence six times.

This sequence provides a gentle way to warm up your spine and get energy flowing through your whole body. The aim is to coordinate your breath and movement, moving slowly and softly – don't rush!

1   2   3   4

WARRIOR POSE
Virabhadrasana

1 Stand with your feet together, arms by your sides.

2 Inhale, turn your right foot outward a little at the toes for stability and step forward with your left foot. Exhale, securely ground your right heel on the floor and balance your weight evenly between your two feet.

3 Breathing in, bend your left knee while simultaneously lifting your arms so that your elbows are bent at shoulder height and your palms face forward. Take three deep breaths in this position. On the final exhalation relax your arms to your sides, straighten your front knee and return to position 2. Finally, step back to the starting position. Repeat the whole exercise on the same side, rest for a few seconds to let your breathing settle completely, then do the sequence twice on the other side.

This dynamic pose helps to lift your energy levels and enhance your mood.

1

2

3

ENERGY MUDRA
Apan Mudra

Doing *apan mudra* helps you to gain a fresh perspective on any troubles and gives you the strength, energy and confidence to move on to new ventures in life. It is also said to help remove waste and toxins from the body.

Sit comfortably and rest your hands on your thighs with your palms facing up. Bring the tips of your middle and ring fingers to contact the tip of your thumb on both hands. Allow your index and little fingers to extend softly. Hold the *mudra* for five to fifteen minutes, two to three times a day, or as you feel you need it.

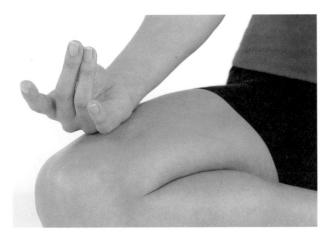

TRIANGLE POSE
Trikonasana

1 Stand with your left foot turned out to ninety degrees and your right foot turned slightly inward. Inhale and lift your arms up to shoulder height with your palms facing down. Keep your shoulders relaxed and wide.

2 Exhale and extend your torso out to your left. Lower your left hand down to your thigh or shin, lift your right arm over your head and broaden the space between your shoulder blades as much as possible. Try to move only sidewise, rather than forward. Look up to your right hand. Inhale and lift yourself back to position 1 and repeat the movement three times on each side.

This posture is a strong side bend that helps to open and stretch the sides of your torso, strengthen your legs, and improve your suppleness and coordination.

TRIANGLE POSE

1

2

45

MIGHTY POSE
Utkatasana

1   Stand with your feet hip-width apart and parallel.

2   Inhale and lift your arms over your head, shoulder-width apart, palms facing each other.

3   Exhale, bend your knees and send your hips backward. Keep your back straight by supporting it with your abdominal muscles. Ensure that your knees track forward over your toes. Now reverse the sequence: inhale, send your hips forward and straighten your legs, then exhale and relax your arms back to your sides. Repeat the whole sequence six times, slowly and steadily.

This is a powerfully invigorating posture that brings increased energy and strengthens both your legs and your breathing. As you practise it, draw strength from the inner core of your body. Allow your breathing to settle once you have finished.

1   2   3

FULL YOGIC BREATHING AND UJJAYI

Here are two simple breathing techniques to help you begin to develop awareness of your breath.

Full yogic breathing

Lie down on your back, close your eyes and breathe through your nose throughout the exercise. Visualize your breath moving into your lower abdominal area — imagine that you fill this whole area with light as you inhale, and free your body from tensions as you exhale. Do this for five to ten breaths. Next, visualize your breath moving into the middle portion of your body (your stomach and lower chest) for another five to ten breaths. Now turn your attention to the upper part of your body (your upper back, collarbones, shoulders, neck, chest, throat and head). Visualize light pouring effortlessly into these areas as you inhale, and let any tension seep away as you exhale (for five to ten breaths).

Now link the three sections of your body as you inhale smoothly. Start by focusing on the lower part of your body, then inhale into the middle part of your body and finally up to the top of your head. As you exhale allow the exhalation to flow down through your body from your head to your lower abdomen. If you notice a slight pause at the top of the inhalation and bottom of the exhalation, let it happen.

Ujjayi

Ujjayi means "victorious". This breathing technique produces a full, strong breath that warms your body and develops your inner strength and will power.

Keeping your mouth softly closed, exhale and inhale through your nose. Slightly contract the muscles in your throat to produce a gentle, continuous hissing sound, rather like the sound of the sea when you put a seashell to your ear. (You will need to use slightly different muscles for the inhalation.) Be careful not to strain your breathing. With practice you will begin to be able to control the length and pressure of each breath extremely accurately. Repeat for twelve breaths at first and increase the number gradually as you gain confidence.

Having perfected the *asanas*, one
should practice *pranayama* according to
the instructions of a teacher, with the
senses under control, observing all
along a nutritious and moderate diet.

HATHAYOGAPRADIPIKA (14TH CENTURY)

When the breath is irregular the
mind is also unsteady, but when
the breath is still, so is the mind.

HATHAYOGAPRADIPIKA (14TH CENTURY)

CAT-DOG-SWAN SEQUENCE

1 Begin on all fours. Inhale and bend your elbows gently back toward your knees as you lift up the centre of your chest, so that your spine curves (this is cat pose). Keep your neck soft and your shoulders rolled back.

2 Breathing out, tuck your toes underneath you and push your hips upward (this is dog pose). Relax your head and neck and keep your shoulders broad and open.

3 Inhale, drop your knees down and return to cat pose.

4 Exhale and gently round your back, tucking your pelvis under you slightly. Now sit back on to your heels, bringing your head to the floor with your hips over your heels (this is swan pose). Repeat the whole sequence six times, breathing steadily throughout.

This sequence increases the energy flow along your spine and reduces tension and stress built up around your neck and shoulders. Be careful not to "do" the poses with your chin — make sure that you integrate the head and neck movements with the rest of your spine.

1

2

3

4

COBRA VARIATIONS

Softer variation

1 Lie face down with your forehead on the floor. Place your hands alongside your ribcage, elbows pointing up.

2 Inhale and lift your head and upper chest. Exhale to return to step 1. Breathe smoothly throughout the movement, keeping your jaw relaxed. Repeat four to six times.

Stronger variation

1 Lie face down with your forehead on the floor and your arms by your sides, palms downward.

2 Inhale and lift your head and chest off the floor. Take your arms out to the sides then all the way round to the front of your head. Exhale, retracing the path of your arms until you return to step 1. Repeat four to six times.

Cobra pose helps to open your chest and strengthen your upper back, which is important if you spend a great deal of time sat at a desk. The pose should not hurt your back — if it does, reduce the degree of movement until it is comfortable for you.

Softer variation

Stronger variation

LEG RAISES
Utthanpadasana

1 Lie on your back with your knees bent and your arms by your sides, palms downward.
2 Exhale and draw your knees in to your chest.
3 Breathing in, simultaneously lift your arms over your head and stretch your legs up (without locking your knees), keeping your belly drawn down to support your spine. Repeat steps 2 and 3 three to six times. Inhale to lower your feet to the floor.

This movement strengthens your lower back and abdominal region and is an excellent antidote to sitting in a chair for a prolonged period of time. Pay special attention to the quality and length of your breath – keep it steady all the way through the posture. You can make the movement easier by doing it with one leg at a time, leaving the other foot on the floor with your knee bent for extra support.

LEG RAISES

1

2

3

ALTERNATE NOSTRIL BREATHING
Alunoma Viloma

This technique manipulates the flow of energy through the *nadi*s (channels) in your body and ultimately brings about a balance of both stimulation and relaxation. Try to make your inhalation and exhalation of equal length and take care not to strain — every breath should be soft and gentle.

Use your right hand to close your nostrils: tuck your index and middle fingers into the palm of your hand, use your thumb to close your right nostril and use your ring and little fingers together to close your left nostril. Close your right nostril and inhale through your left nostril (see opposite, above). Now close your left nostril, release your thumb and exhale through your right nostril. Now inhale through your right nostril (see opposite, below). Close your right nostril with your thumb, release your fingers and exhale through your left nostril to complete one round of *alunoma viloma*. Begin with eight rounds and build up to doing sixteen.

TWISTING POSE
Jathara Parivriti

1 Lie on your back with your arms stretched out at shoulder level. Bend your knees and place your feet flat on the floor. Lift your left leg up toward the ceiling.

2 Exhale and carefully lower your left leg across to the right side of your body. If possible, catch hold of your toes with your right hand. Gently turn your head to look over your left shoulder. Stay in this position for four to six full, steady breaths. Repeat twice on both your left and right side.

Twisting poses invigorate the whole spine, increasing the flow of prana *and stimulating the nervous system. They are also particularly good for the digestive system and give tone and condition to the internal organs.*

BRIDGE POSE

1 Lie on your back with your knees bent and your feet flat on the floor, parallel and hip-width apart. Sink your feet firmly into the ground and keep your big toes in contact with the floor.

2 Inhale and lift your hips off the floor. Draw your shoulders together, clasp your hands underneath you and gently push your hands toward your heels. Tilt your pelvis upward to lift your hips a little further. Keep your knees parallel. Breathe fully into your chest area for three to six breaths. To come out of the pose, release your hands and spread your arms out. As you exhale, lower your spine on to the floor one vertebra at a time. Rest until your breathing settles. Repeat the whole sequence two to four times.

This invigorating backbend broadens your chest and strengthens your legs and abdominal area. Do the pose mindfully – notice the symmetrical balance of the posture as the back and front of your body draw together to support one another.

1

2

ON INNER STRENGTH

This meditation focuses on the root *chakra* (*muladhara chakra*), the energy centre in our body that connects us to earth, and brings a sense of stability (see page 29).

1 Sit in a comfortable position with your spine straight. Place your hands palms down on your knees or thighs and close your eyes. Take a few moments to focus on your body: release any tense muscles and let yourself spread out to your full sitting height and width – feel solid and stable in your position.

2 Focus on your breathing. As you inhale draw strength from the ground up into your body. With each out-breath you grow a little more solid, stable and strong.

3 Allow your mind to settle on the innate stability and strength of your inner self. If you notice other thoughts drifting into your mind, gently refocus on your breath. After a few minutes return your focus to your body. Become aware of the weight of your body. Sit quietly like this for a few moments before getting up.

The state of Yoga can be reached
by persevering practice
and non-attachment.

PATANJALI

YOGA SUTRAS (*c*.200BCE–*c*.200CE)

The mind becomes settled when it cultivates
friendliness in the face of happiness,
compassion in the face of misery,
joy in the face of virtue,
and indifference in the face of error.

PATANJALI

YOGA SUTRAS (*c*.200BCE–*c*.200CE)

Chapter Three

yoga relaxation

It seems that most of us experience excessive stress in our lives at some stage. This is hardly surprising given the "unnatural" life most of us lead — one in which we are separated from our body's natural rhythms and bombarded with sensory messages. Consider: almost all of us are woken every morning by an alarm clock, and are shortly afterward launched into the stress of rush-hour traffic, constant noise and pollution. For recreation we make more demands of our nervous systems by going to the cinema (think of the emotions you experience while seeing a horror movie or thriller!), watching television, or listening to music. Stress can take other forms, too: isolation and boredom can be as stressful for our body and mind as overstimulation. The overall result, of course, is that we lose touch with our innate sense of peace.

Yoga is renowned for its calming effects. In fact, yoga is a powerful tool to help you break the cycle of stress, relax your mind and body, and nourish your nervous system to keep it healthy and balanced. This chapter presents techniques that will help you to focus inwardly. They will help you to release yourself from the external causes of stress and to return to a place of stillness at your centre. Practise each suggestion in sequence in the order given, or individually as best suits your needs.

YOGA BRINGS YOU CALM

Stress is not always a bad thing – in fact, we all need a little to keep us motivated. However, this "optimum" level of stress is different for each of us. Think about your own optimum level – under what amount of pressure do you feel that you accomplish most? For some this might be when the day is filled with activity, seemingly without a minute spare; for others, it might be when demands are made in short, concise bursts, with long periods of calm in between. There is no competition here – your optimum stress level is individual to you, and there is nothing to be gained by competing with someone else apparently to "outdo" them. Recognize your personal limit.

The body reflects our state of mind. If we are under pressure (or angry), our bodies perceive danger and prepare for what is known as the "fight-or-flight" response. Our muscles tighten and the body physically primes itself for defensive action – or for a quick getaway! If you are sitting at your desk or driving through heavy traffic and you get frustrated, upset or angry, the fight-or-flight reponse kicks in. However, because the threat posed is not something that you can (in the physical sense) attack or escape from, your stress is not released. After a while, your body will assume permanently the shape of the fight-or-flight reflex: the telltale signs of hunched shoulders, a clenched stomach, gritted teeth, and short, shallow breathing.

To counter this we need a reliable practice that will enable the body to release pent-up pressure. Yoga is well known for its calming effects. Posture practice moves our muscles gently out of their fixed patterns of tension, and thus helps to release the muscle tightness associated with stress. As your breathing slows down and deepens through posture and meditation practice, your nervous system will return to a state of relaxation. However, the ability to tap into instant calm will not come straightaway. Persevere with the techniques in this chapter. After a while yoga practice will help to develop new patterns of response in you: a more flexible and open posture encourages a more flexible and open mind.

THE SEAL OF WISDOM
AND THE SEAL OF KNOWLEDGE
Jnana Mudra and Chin Mudra

These *mudra*s are used in many traditions of meditation practice worldwide. They are said to aid the channelling of energy into the higher *chakra*s, thus lifting us into subtler states of consciousness – you may experience lightness in your spine, chest and head. Both of them can also induce a more solid, grounding feeling and are said to aid memory and bring mental focus.

Bring the tips of your index finger and your thumb together (as shown opposite) on both hands. Rest your hands on your knees, palms facing up for *jnana mudra* (see opposite, above), or facing down for *chin mudra* (see opposite, below). Practise either mudra for five to fifteen minutes at a time, once or twice a day, or use them as an aid to meditation or breathing practice. Try moving from one *mudra* to the other to become aware of the different effect each one has on you.

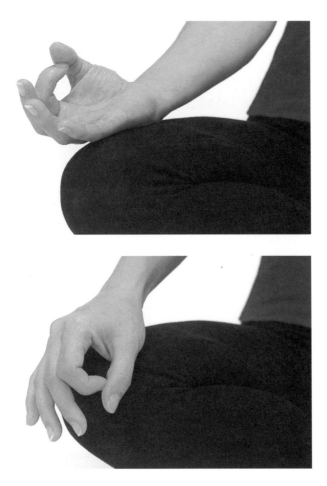

RELAXATION POSTURES

Try these relaxation poses for between three and fifteen minutes or more. They make a great way to wind down after work.

Lower-back rest Lie on the floor with a cushion or rolled-up blanket under your knees. Place your hands on your lower abdominal area. This posture relieves lower-back pain, fatigue and tension and helps you to feel "centred".

Chest-opener Use a large bolster or firmly rolled blanket to rest your upper body on. Relax your arms to the sides, palms facing up. If your lower back feels overstretched, add a little extra padding under your hips. This is a great way to counter upper-back and neck tension. If you are very tense, this pose may feel too dramatic, in which case opt for a different pose.

Supported child pose Place a large cushion or bolster between your knees to support you in a forward bending pose – use enough padding to feel really comfortable. Simply rest your head and relax your arms by your side.

Lower-back rest

Chest-opener

Supported child pose

FORWARD BEND
Uttanasana

1 Stand with your feet hip-width apart and parallel. Broaden and relax your shoulders by rolling them back and down. Lengthen and soften the back of your neck.

2 As you breathe in lift your arms over your head. You can do this either by bringing them up in front of you or by drawing them out to the sides.

3 Exhale and fold your body forward. Bring your hands down toward your feet and bend your knees as much as you need in order to relax your torso, head and neck. Reverse the movement. Inhale and come back up to position 2, lifting your arms out in front of you if you are strong enough, or, opening them out to the sides, which is a little easier. As you exhale relax your arms to your sides (position 1). Repeat four to six times.

This simple movement is beneficial for the spine and internal organs. Furthermore, concentrating on the flow of breath and movement in this sequence brings us a more positive outlook.

1   2   3

FLANK FORWARD BEND
Parsva Uttanasana

1 Stand with your left foot forward and your right foot turned out slightly. Inhale and lift your arms overhead. Lengthen your spine and allow your tailbone to drop down. Keep your back foot fully grounded for stability.

2 As you breathe out, gently fold forward. Bend your left knee a little, even if you are flexible enough to fold forward with your leg straight. Place your hands palms down on the floor on either side of your foot and totally relax your head and neck. Take one full breath: inhale to expand your upper back and chest gently; exhale to release. Breathing in, keep your spine straight as you draw yourself back up to position 1. As you breathe out, relax your arms to your sides. Repeat three times on each side.

This is a wonderful way of shedding burdens! Think of a rucksack full of everything you no longer want to carry with you — as you fold forward, let its contents tumble out.

1   2

HUMMING BEE BREATH
Bhramari

The sound created in this breathing exercise is just like that of a bumble bee. Humming creates a vibration in your body that is wonderfully soothing and nurturing. This technique will help to calm your nerves and bring you an overall sense of well-being.

Sit in a comfortable position with your eyes closed and take a few seconds to turn your attention inward to your breath. If you wish, you can gently block your ears with your fingers. Take a long, steady inhalation. On the exhalation hum gently, keeping your jaw relaxed. Continue to hum on every exhalation, allowing the sound to vibrate in the different areas of your face and head. Experiment with different pitches until you find one that feels comfortable for you – the sound should be smooth, resonant and full. Stay with this breathing technique for eight to twelve complete breaths (in and out), then sit quietly for a while, listening to your breath and the "after-hum" of the vibration.

KNEELING-CAT-SWAN POSE

1 Kneel down with your hands on your thighs, eyes closed.

2 As you breathe in, gently lift your arms overhead and come up to a raised kneeling position.

3 As you breathe out, gently bring your hands to the floor in front of you and softly curve your spine upward.

4 Inhale, bend your elbows and lift the centre of your chest forward and upward (this is cat pose).

5 As you breathe out, tilt your pelvis under you and curve your spine to sit back with your hips over your heels. This is swan pose. Inhale to return to position 1 and exhale to relax your shoulders. Repeat the whole sequence six times.

This sequence is a soft and gentle way to release tension from your spine, clear your head and calm your nerves. Try to complete the series of postures with your eyes closed. Listen carefully to the duration and quality of your breath, and allow each change of posture to be initiated by the start of either your next inhalation or next exhalation.

1

2

3

4

5

SQUATTING POSE

1 Turn your feet slightly outward, bend your knees and
   adopt a deep squatting position. (If you find it difficult
   to squat comfortably, place a block or a book under both
   heels, as shown.) Make sure your insteps are not rolling
   forward – this can stress your knee joints. Palms together, gently press your elbows into the insides of your
   knees. Stay for a few breaths.

2 Clasp your hands, place your thumbs on top of your
   fingers and gently rest your forehead on your thumbs.
   Close your eyes and rock gently back and forth for a few
   minutes, gradually reducing the movement until you are
   still again. Softly lift your head and neck to straighten
   your back, and then open your eyes.

*Many of us in the West are stiff in the hips, knees and ankles
because we sit on furniture from a young age. Squatting helps
to lengthen your lower back and keep your knees, ankles and
hips supple and strong. Practise this posture for a few minutes
a day to improve your flexibility and general posture.*

1

2

INNER HARMONY MUDRA
Matangi mudra

Matangi mudra helps to create a sense of balance and harmony in your mind and body. Practising this *mudra* also brings a quality of repose and ease if you are feeling fragile or overstimulated, and helps to settle your breath and quieten down your mind. Furthermore, this *mudra* is said to assist the flow of energy in the internal organs around the solar plexus (stomach area).

Clasp your hands together and place them at the level of your solar plexus. Now release your two middle fingers, extend them and bring them together to form a point. Hold this *mudra* for a few minutes. Try to practise the *mudra* two to three times a day or use it whenever you feel you need "balancing".

HEAD-TO-KNEE POSE
Janu Sirsanana

1 Sit on the floor, or on a small block or cushion to lift your hips slightly. Extend both legs, then bend your right knee so that your right foot touches your left thigh. If your right knee is a long way from the floor, prop it up with a cushion. Breathing in, lift your arms over your head with your palms facing each other and lengthen the whole of your spine.

2 As you breathe out, lower your hands to the floor on either side of your left knee (or your shin or foot if they are easy to reach). Relax your torso as you fold forward toward your extended leg. Inhale and return to position 1. Repeat this sequence four times. Then, on the fifth round, stay in position 2 for four breaths. Now repeat the whole sequence on the other side.

This posture stimulates the spine and internal organs. Bowing your head down is also a gesture of relinquishing your burdens and "letting go", both physically and mentally.

HEAD-TO-KNEE POSE

1

2

TWO GENTLE TWISTS

Sacral spine twist

1 Lie on your back with your knees bent and your feet flat on the floor, knees and feet together. Rest your arms outward at shoulder level, palms facing up.

2 As you breathe out drop your knees over to the right side. Stay like this for six to eight breaths. Inhale to return to position 1 and repeat on the other side.

Lumbar spine twist

1 Lie on your back and draw your knees toward your chest. Rest your arms outward at shoulder level, palms up.

2 Exhale, drop your knees to the right and turn your head to the left. Stay like this for six to eight breaths. Inhale to return to position 1 and repeat on the other side.

The sacral spine twist concentrates on the lower abdomen and lowest part of the back (an area where many of us hold tension); the lumbar spine twist is a good way to relieve lower-back stiffness and ease digestive problems.

Sacral spine twist

1

2

Lumbar spine twist

1

2

BRIDGE POSE/KNEES-TO-CHEST POSE
Dwi pada Pitham/Apanasana

Bridge pose

1 Lie on your back with your arms by your sides and your feet on the floor, knees bent.

2 Inhale, lift your arms over your head and raise your hips. Exhale and bring your arms and hips back to return to position 1. Repeat six times.

Knees-to-chest pose

1 Lie on your back. Exhaling, draw your knees toward your chest. Place your hands on your knees, elbows tucked in.

2 As you inhale, lift your knees away from your chest until your arms are more or less straight. Repeat six times or more or less as you need.

These postures massage your spine and release tension from your shoulders, lengthening the back and front of the body in turn. Practise them in sequence as a "mini" yoga practice before bedtime — keep your eyes closed throughout.

Bridge pose

Knees-to-chest pose

SLEEPING AND WAKING

When we are in a deep sleep, we are said to be closer to our inner self and that which is holy within us. Many people often suffer from bouts of insomnia or restless sleep when they are suffering from stress or anxiety. For a few people this problem can become chronic, resulting in fatigue and depression. Whether you do have insomnia or would just like to ensure a good night's sleep, the yoga techniques listed below can help you to sleep deeply and wake up feeling refreshed.

Postures for sleep Resting poses such as forward bends (see page 76) and gentle twists (see page 90), or any of the relaxation postures on page 74 present the ideal prelude to sleep. Avoid strong back-bending postures.

Breathing for sleep A few rounds of *ujjayi* breathing (see page 49) or alternate nostril breathing (see page 58) will balance your body's energetic system, bringing deep, peaceful sleep.

Mudra for sleep: shakti mudra Practise *shakti mudra* before bedtime to help you to wind down and relax. Tuck your thumbs into your palms, curl your index and middle fingers around them and bring your hands together so that the tips of your little and ring fingers touch. Allow your breathing and thoughts to slow down and close your eyes. Rest peacefully like this for five to ten minutes.

Waking up We often complain about feeling groggy in the morning. Try this routine before you get up to help you to feel more refreshed: pinch around the outside edge of your ears; interlace your fingers, turn your hands palms outward and lift them over your head; stretch your body, yawn and take several deep breaths.

Here are some other things to try to help you to sleep well. Go to bed at a regular time. Avoid drinking alcohol, coffee, tea or anything with stimulants in it (including chocolate). Don't eat just before bedtime – going to bed on a full stomach does not help you to sleep. Try drinking camomile tea or a glass of warm milk with a pinch of nutmeg in it. Have a "quiet time" for an hour or so before you go to bed – turn off your television or radio and perhaps look at the stars for a moment before turning in.

95

YOGIC SLEEP
Yoga Nidra

Yoga nidra (yogic sleep) is a form of very deep relaxation in which your mind remains conscious, but your entire body relaxes completely as if you were asleep.

Before you begin *yoga nidra*, ensure that your room is warm and well ventilated. Then lie on your back with your legs stretched out a few inches apart and your arms resting palms up, about ten inches from your hips. You may want to cover yourself with a blanket because your body temperature drops as you relax. (If your lower back is uncomfortable, place a cushion under your knees, or bend your knees and rest the soles of your feet on the floor.) In *yoga nidra* you simply rotate your awareness around your body. Don't consciously try to relax – just follow the instructions in the exercise (you could record them on to tape and play them back to yourself if it helps).

Become aware of your left foot and your lower left leg (your shin and calf muscle), the front and back of your left knee, your thigh, hip socket and pelvis. Focus on your hip socket again and reverse the order of your focus of attention as you go back down your leg. Repeat on your right leg. Relax your abdominal area so that it becomes soft, and release your buttock muscles so that you sink into the floor. Now focus on each individual vertebra in your spine from your coccyx (the base of your spine) to your neck. Place your attention on the sound of your heartbeat. Monitor the movement of breath in your ribcage for a few moments. Become aware of your left hand: your palm, thumb and fingers. Move your attention to your left wrist, forearm, elbow, upper arm, shoulder and collarbone, then move down your arm once more. Repeat on your right side. Now turn your attention to the muscles in your scalp, forehead, cheeks, eyelids, lips, jaw and throat. Let your tongue come away from the roof of your mouth. Sense the movement of breath in your nostrils. Allow your eyes to relax deep down into their sockets and feel your head resting on the floor. Simply let your mind and body be still. Stay here quietly for a few minutes. Slowly come up to sitting.

RELAXING BREATHING SEQUENCE

1. Lie on your back with your knees raised and your feet flat on the floor, hip-width apart. Rest your arms by your sides, palms down. Close your eyes.

2. Inhale and raise both your arms to vertical. Now exhale to relax your shoulders heavily into the floor.

3. Inhale and lift your right arm over your head; exhale to bring it back to position 2.

4. Inhale and lift your left arm over your head; exhale to bring it back to position 2.

5. Inhale and move both your arms out to the sides; exhale and let them rest on the floor. Then inhale and lift your arms back to position 2; exhale and return your arms to position 1. Repeat the whole exercise four to eight times and then relax for a few moments and allow your mind and body to be completely still.

This set of arm movements combined with deep, steady breathing is an ideal way to unwind and relax after a stressful day – it relieves tension in your shoulders, neck and jaw.

ON INNER HARMONY

This meditation focuses on the heart centre, the location of the *anahata chakra* (see page 29). This *chakra* is associated with peace and loving compassion.

1 Sit in a comfortable position. Bring your index finger and thumb together into *chin mudra* (see page 72). Close your eyes. Breathe slowly and steadily for a few minutes with *ujjayi* breath (see page 49).

2 Release any tension in your lower back by lengthening your spine and relaxing your shoulders. Broaden your chest, soften your face, release your jaw, dip your chin slightly toward your throat, and relax your inner thighs.

3 Now turn your attention to the centre of your body – your heart. Focus on the sense of peace there: as you inhale visualize light radiating out from your heart, soaking into every cell in your body; as you exhale draw light toward your heart from the surface of your skin. After a few minutes bring your palms together and stay like this for a moment or two before opening your eyes.

Before yoga is taught, the teacher should consider
the time, the surroundings, age, nature of employment,
energy and strength of the person.

[...]

Because all bodies are different, all the *asanas* are
not meant for everybody.

[...]

Great sages, having examined the needs of all types
of people, proposed many *asanas*. Among them,
whatever is suitable must be understood and the
appropriate *asanas* must be taught.

SRI NATHAMUNI

(9TH CENTURY)

Chapter Four

yoga living

Yoga is not simply a system of exercises. Yoga can also be a method by which you harmonize all aspects of yourself (mind, body and spirit) and your life – no matter what your situation. Being able to sit in lotus position does not make you "good" at yoga (which is one of the reasons why the lotus does not even appear in this book). The aim in yoga is not to achieve a perfect posture, but to be willing and able to carry through into your daily life what you learn about yourself during your yoga practice. For this reason it is important not to compare your experience of yoga with someone else's, but instead simply to follow your intuition about what is right for you.

In this chapter you will find two ways to expand the work you do with the postures, which together provide a rounded guide to living a healthy, happy and balanced life. First, there is a description of the social and ethical principles of yoga – understanding them will help you to carry the spirit of yoga into all aspects of your life. Second, we take an introductory look at yoga's "twin sister" Ayurveda, a healing tradition from India. Through Ayurveda you are able to observe, recognize and account for the qualities that make you who you are. With this knowledge you will be able to alter your daily routine and yoga practice to suit your individual constitution.

USING YOGA IN THE EVERYDAY WORLD

Patanjali's *Yoga Sutras* (*c.*200BCE–*c.*200CE) describes an eight-step path to yoga, known as the Eight Limbs of yoga. The first two limbs are *yama* and *niyama*, the social and personal principles by which we should live our lives to move closer to a state of self-realization. The next two limbs are *asana* (postures) and *pranayama* (breathing techniques), already explored in previous chapters. The last four are *pratyahara* (withdrawal of the senses), *dharana* (concentration), *dhyana* (meditation) and *samadhi* (the super-conscious state).

In order truly to begin to integrate yoga into our everyday lives, we need to gain a fuller understanding of the first two limbs. While we cannot hope to adopt all the ethical principles of *yama* (see pages 108–109) and *niyama* (see pages 110–113) in one go, we should aim gradually to introduce them. Little by little they may become a framework of universal ideals that can support and enrich your life, ultimately leading to your spiritual growth and development.

YAMA

The following are the five *yama* of social conduct – the first limb of yoga.

Non-violence ahimsa

The first and most important of the *yama* is *ahimsa*, or non-violence. *Ahimsa* is not only an instruction to stop you injuring another person – it includes non-violence to the environment and even to yourself. Begin *ahimsa* by respecting your health – eat foods that are good for you and avoid any unsuitable exercise that may cause damage to your body (this extends to unsuitable use of yoga postures and breathing exercises).

Truthfulness satya

Although being truthful may seem simple, it often requires great courage. We should try to speak only the truth. If this is not possible without causing harm, we should remain silent. *Satya* also demands that we look deeply into ourselves to find the truth about who we are.

Non-stealing asteya

We should not take that which does not belong to us. The principle should be applied as much to others' time and good will as to their possessions. In your yoga practice make sure that you do not "rob" one part of your posture to improve another (for example, do not do a posture so strongly that you cannot breathe properly).

Moderation brahmacarya

Moderation in all things produces a harmonious lifestyle. We are often invited to overindulge, but remember that too much of anything can be bad for you. Nothing is positive in excess, not even yoga postures!

Non-greed aparigraha

Aparigraha (also translated as "non-grasping"), describes a state where we have what we need and use it wisely without grasping for more. Begin using this *yama* in your yoga practice. Rather than trying to do your yoga postures "better", concentrate on doing them mindfully, without anticipating the results or rewards.

NIYAMA

Niyama, the second limb of yoga, are five interdependent principles concerned with your personal conduct.

Cleanliness sauca

Our first duty toward ourselves is to keep our body and mind healthy and strong. Cleanliness not only keeps the body healthy, it also symbolizes washing away impurity from the mind and spirit. Ideally you should wash before and after posture practice. Yoga postures help to keep your internal systems clean and well nourished. We can extend the practice of *sauca* to our surroundings. Keeping the place in which we live well maintained helps us to function more effectively in our daily lives, and shows respect for our environment.

Contentment samtosa

Contentment is having a positive attitude toward everything in your life (past, present and future), seeing your glass as "half-full" rather than as "half-empty". This attitude can be difficult to foster in the West, for we are continually encouraged to judge ourselves and others by what we have in terms of possessions and wealth. This can foster emotions such as envy. However, being content does not mean we should not strive to improve our situation or change things that are unjust. We should try to free ourselves from any kind of greed or material ambition; enrich our sense of self and be content with what we have, material or otherwise.

Discipline tapas

Discipline is not fashionable. You may reject the idea of *tapas* as unappealing – even brutal. However, through living a disciplined life we are able to be moderate in all things and live a life of balance. Moderation, you remember, is one of the five *yama* of social conduct (*brahmacarya*). Think practically about discipline. For example, boring tasks that need to be done, such as changing the washer on the bathroom tap, niggle at us, yet we often put them off in favour of more enjoyable ways of spending our time. Change the washer! Mow the

lawn! Fix the drawer! And do these tasks with a smile –
in doing so, life will seem better all round.

Self-study swadhyaya

Traditionally *swadhyaya* would have been the study of
yogic texts. For those of us who are not devoting our lives
so fully to yoga, there is still valuable instruction in
swadhyaya. Think of the practice simply as an encour-
agement to further your understanding of yourself.
You could do this by enrolling for an evening class of
your choice, learning a new skill, or reading a book of
a spiritual nature. If you live a hectic, overpopulated
lifestyle, take some time out for solitary self-reflection.
Self-study need not be onerous – for example, you could
just spend an evening reading an uplifting book (such as
a biography of a spiritual leader) instead of reading a
work of fiction. Investing even short amounts of time on
your personal development can lead you to experiences
that you never imagined you would have, and to a level of
understanding of yourself and of the world that you
thought unattainable.

Devotion isvarapranidhana

The last of the *niyama*s is devotion to "the highest" (Patanjali does not use the word God because the *Yoga Sutras* is not a specifically religious text). If you have a religious belief, you can use your yoga practice as an act of devotion to your God. However, *isvarapranidhana* also offers something important for those of us without any religious belief. If this includes you, where do you imagine you will find the ultimate truth? What or who represents the highest form of universal knowledge for you? Perhaps you can devote your practice to, say, Mother Nature, some kind of universal consciousness, or even an inner spirit that lies deep within yourself. If you are not sure what you consider to be "the highest", don't despair. Just try to open your mind to the wonders of the world. Try to spend a short time each day in appreciation of something you find inspirational, such as a person who has done great things, a magnificent mountain, a beautiful work of art, the boundlessness of the night sky, or a tiny plant growing through the cracks in the concrete.

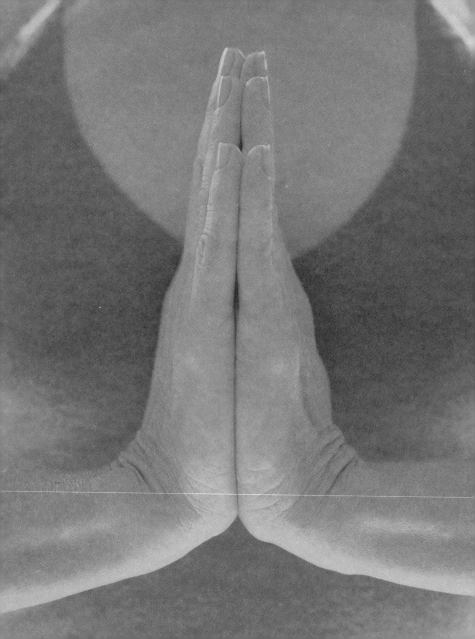

Truth should be told when agreeable,
should be said agreeably, and truth
should not be said that does harm;
however, never lie to give pleasure.

VYASA

MAHABHARATA (6TH CENTURY BCE)

When your mind is free from clouds
that prevent clear perception, you transcend
limitations and your consciousness expands.
Knowledge becomes infinite and there is
nothing more to be known.

PATANJALI

YOGA SUTRAS (*c.*200BCE–*c.*200CE)

AYURVEDA AND DOSHIC TYPES

While yoga is primarily a system for bringing about greater awareness and eventually self-realization, Ayurveda is concerned with self-healing. The words *ayur veda* mean the "science of life". Essentially, Ayurveda (which has evolved alongside yoga over thousands of years) is a method of prescribing natural remedies according to an individual's constitution (*dosha*).

In Ayurveda there are three basic types of *dosha* known as *vata*, *pitta* and *kapha*. These qualities apply not only to your physical body, but also to your mind and emotions. Your doshic constitution (that is, the ratio of the three *dosha*s within you) is unique to you and determined at your conception. Usually, one of the *dosha*s will predominate over the others. You can determine your doshic type (find your predominant *dosha*) by using the simple chart on pages 118–19. Complete the chart by assessing the whole of your life, not just how you are feeling today. (For a really accurate reading, it is best to consult an Ayurvedic practitioner.)

Once you know your doshic type, you can adjust your yoga practice, diet and other aspects of your life to complement it. You will feel more balanced, and draw upon your strengths, if you can "pacify" your predominant *dosha*, and enhance the qualities of the other *dosha*s. The food lists and posture lists (pages 120–123) suggest changes you can make to your diet and yoga practice to balance your *dosha*s. Follow the guidelines for your doshic type.

To prevent illness you should try to avoid activities or circumstances that intensify the qualities of your doshic type. *Vata* qualities are cold, dry, light, rough and mobile. *Vata*-types, prone to digestive problems, should avoid such things as exposure to the cold, too much dry food, too much travelling or a lack or routine. *Pitta* qualities are hot, light, moist, oily and sharp. *Pitta*-types should avoid *pitta*-increasing factors such as hot weather and/or too much alcohol and spicy food. *Kapha* qualities are heavy, cold, moist, soft and firm. *Kapha*-increasing factors include eating and sleeping too much, lack of exercise, and exposure to cold weather.

DETERMINE YOUR DOSHIC TYPE

To determine your doshic type, count how many "ticks" you get for each *dosha* in the chart below. The *dosha* with the most ticks predominates. If two suggestions in a doshic category apply equally, tick both. If none of the suggestions in a category applies, tick none.

	Vata	Pitta	Kapha
Height	tall, short	medium	stocky, tall
Build	thin, bony	medium	large, heavy
Weight	light	medium	heavy
Skin	dull, dry, thin	warm, freckles	pale, moist
Face shape	thin, long, oval	heart-shape	round or square
Eyes	small, brown	piercing	large
Lips	thin, dry	soft, pink	pale, cold
Nose	thin, long	sharp, pointed	straight, thick
Tongue	dry, rough	red, dark	white
Hair	dry, thin, curly	oily, thin, bald	thick, wavy, oily
Teeth	crooked	medium, yellow	large, even

Nails	rough, brittle	soft, pink	soft, white, firm
Joints	stiff, cracking	flexible	firm, strong
Sweating	little	profuse	moderate
Sleep	poor, fitful	little but sound	excessive
Dreams	frequent	moderate	rare, disturbed
Endurance	poor	moderate	excellent
Speech	fast, frequent	clear, abrupt	slow, melodious
Memory	poor long-term	good, sharp	good long-term
Lifestyle	erratic	busy	steady
Sexuality	can be cold	intense	warm, constant
Appetite	needs frequent, small meals	good, strong digestion	likes spicy foods
Worst qualities	anxious, indecisive,	angry, irritable, arrogant	lazy, greedy, stubborn
Best qualities	active, creative	sensitive, compassionate	calm, stable, dependable
Common ailments	dandruff, constipation	rashes, allergic reactions	sore throats, headaches
Possible career	musicians, teachers	leaders, directors	doctors, accountants

FOOD LISTS

Vata

Eat more: dairy products, especially goat's milk; nuts, tofu, mung beans, rice, oats, wheat, cooked vegetables.
Avoid: dried fruits, apples, melons, cranberries, hard cheese, frozen vegetables, white sugar, chocolate, and anything gas-forming, including most pulses.

Pitta

Eat more: soft cheese, ice cream, yogurt, beet, asparagus, raw vegetables, cereals, beans and pulses.
Avoid: lemons, grapefruit, salted butter, hard cheese, sour cream, horseradish, garlic, peppers and nuts.

Kapha

Eat more: apples, pears, low-fat soft cheese, sunflower seeds, popcorn, barley, rye and honey.
Avoid: banana, kiwi, watermelon, squash, pumpkin, tomatoes, cucumber, butter, ice cream, full-fat yogurt, avocado, nuts, rice, wheat, oats and iced water.

POSTURE LISTS

Vata

Vata people should concentrate on postures that bring steadiness and stability to their yoga practice. Forward bending postures such as forward bend (page 76) and flank forward bend (page 78) are particularly useful if you do them slowly and methodically. The sequence on page 82 is calming for *vata*-types. Gentle back bending, particularly in the upper spine area, is also good – try poses such as cobra (page 54), bridge (page 62) or the chest-opener on page 74. Sitting postures that emphasize stability (such as squatting pose, page 84) can also help. Be careful not to overstretch or do too vigorous a practice. Ensure that your breath remains slow and steady throughout your practice.

Pitta

Pitta people need to ensure that they do not become overcompetitive or push themselves too hard in their yoga. In your practice emphasize postures that invert your body, such as dog pose (step 2 of the sequence on page 52). *Pitta*-types also benefit from all the twisting postures (pages 60 and 90) and forward bends (pages 76 and 78) when performed moderately and with care. Avoid getting too hot and sweaty in your practice. Make sure that you rest between each pose so that your breath returns to normal. Try practising *yoga nidra* (pages 96–7) or alternate nostril breathing (page 58) in the early morning or the evening.

Kapha

Kapha people need to keep moving. Ideally you should break into a gentle sweat from doing your practice and your body should feel warm and light. Minimize seated postures and instead place emphasis on all the standing postures, such as mountain pose (page 36), warrior pose (page 40) and sequences such as cat-dog-swan sequence (page 52). Use your yoga practice to get you going in the mornings. You may find that you are not as flexible as you would like to be. Don't worry just keep moving and your body will loosen over time.

Removing impurity through
continued practice of the Eight
Limbs of Yoga brings discernment
and clear perception.

PATANJALI

YOGA SUTRAS (*c.*200BCE–*c.*200CE)

The Eight Limbs of Yoga are:
attitudes toward others, attitudes
toward ourselves, postures,
breath control, detaching at will
from the senses, concentration,
meditation, and integration with
the object to be understood.

PATANJALI

YOGA SUTRAS (*c.*200BCE–*c.*200CE)

INDEX

Picture Credits

The publisher would like to thank the following people, museums and photographic libraries for permission to reproduce their material. Every care has been taken to trace copyright holders. However, if we have omitted anyone we apologise and will, if informed, make corrections in any future edition.

Page 2 AKG; **14** Photonica/Jun Kishimoto; **31** Bruce Coleman Collection; **50** Stone/Getty One; **64** Photonica/Shinzo Hirai; **67** Stone/Getty Images; **80** Corbis/Mike Zens; **100** Bruce Coleman Collection; **103** Ray Massey Photography; **107** FPG/Getty Images; **114** Stone/Getty Images; **121** Waitrose Food Illustrated/Fleur Olby; **125** Bruce Coleman Collection

Author's Acknowledgment

I would like to thank Anna Roseveare for her unfailing support and enthusiasm.

Publisher's Acknowledgments

Model: Suzy Barton
Make-up artist: Lizzie Lawson

Tara Fraser can be contacted at her yoga school:
Yoga Junction at The Whittington Park Community Centre
Yerbury Road
London
N19 4RS
020 7263 3113
www.yogajunction.com